THIS NOTEBOOK BELONGS TO ....

CONTACT ....

See our range of fine, illustrated books, ebooks, notebooks and art calendars:
www.flametreepublishing.com

This is a **FLAME TREE NOTEBOOK**
Published and © copyright 2018 Flame Tree Publishing Ltd

FTNB176 • 978-1-78755-015-5

Cover image based on a detail from
Golden Buddha
© one AND only/Shutterstock.com

Like in many other statues of Buddha, the spiritual leader is
shown in the lotus position used in meditation. As one of the
basic teachings of Buddhism, meditation is a way of gaining
insight into one's mind and achieving inner calm. The practice
has now spread widely, being utilised in yoga or even as a
technique to reduce the effects of depression and anxiety.

FLAME TREE PUBLISHING | The Art of Fine Gifts
6 Melbray Mews, London SW6 3NS, United Kingdom